Las Vegas Books   **$7.99**
Segall, Ma/How to Make Love to
(BUS) /Floor   10/27/22 / HC

9 789910 588549

HOW TO MAKE LOVE
TO YOUR MONEY

HOW TO MAKE LOVE
TO YOUR MONEY

BY MARK SEGALL AND MARGARET TOBIN

DESIGNED AND ILLUSTRATED BY MARC ROSENTHAL

Delacorte Press/New York

Published by
Delacorte Press
1 Dag Hammarskjold Plaza
New York, N.Y. 10017

Manufactured in the United States of America

First printing

Type set by Jack Godler Associates

Library of Congress Cataloging in Publication Data
Segall, Mark.
    How to make love to your money.

    1. Finance, Personal—Anecdotes, facetiae, etc.
2. Investments—Ancedotes, facetiae, etc.
I. Tobin, Margaret.   II. Title.
HG179.S39 1982   332.024'00207   82-12705
ISBN 0-440-03357-8

CREDIT WHERE CREDIT IS DUE

Our thanks and long-term appreciation to:
Marcia Wooding Caro
Ellen Milhan Klein
Michael A. J. Kozlowski
Caroline Minori
Bruce Rafferty
Herman Schonbrun
Martin Spindel
Cynthia Vartan
Susan Zeckendorf
and
David Freedman
Eileen Rosenberg

CHAPTER ONE

HOW TO
SURVIVE
THE
FIDUCIOSEXUAL
REVOLUTION

he sixties opened up new frontiers of consciousness, self-consciousness, and unconsciousness; of rampant hetero-, homo-, and bisexuality. In the seventies everybody took a break and watched Watergate on TV. But by 1979 rumblings of a new epoch were felt in the same social laboratory that had spawned the Love Generation—California. There Howard Jarvis boldly propositioned the entire voting-age population to strip off their taxes, shed their social consciences, and roll shamelessly in dough. The Aquarian Age was over. The Golden Age had just begun.

9

In 1980 another Californian, a twice-married former screen star with pomaded hair and twinkling eyes, simply seduced a country with shameless promises of lower deficits, supply-side stimulation, and a sinfully well-endowed war machine. Once in office he unleashed the passions of large corporate bodies. Formerly staid financial institutions started merging with each other, frantically stripping one another's assets. The Fiduciosexual Revolution was in full swing.

The average citizen was mystified. All his life he had believed the conventional wisdom: "'Nice' boys and girls don't fool around with funds," "Money can't buy you love," and "The best things in life are free." But now, all around him, he saw people he respected and admired indulging in profligate profiteering. Even his President was openly advocating "free markets."

These trends came as a shock to someone who had always viewed money as a necessary evil, something that just helped him "get by," "a measure of value or a medium of exchange," or "what rich people have." The average American felt out of it, behind the times. What was going on? What had become of the old values? And most important, how could he get a piece of the action?

One answer lies in the work of Drs. Georgia S. Boodle and Myron F. Scheckel, two scientists who have profited handsomely by helping people adjust to the changing times. Recently their Foundation for Fiduciosexual Fulfillment won a multimillion-dollar government grant to develop cash therapies for fiscal dysfunction. Less fortunate scientists in established fields like cancer research reacted angrily, calling Boodle and Scheckel "moneygrubbing charlatans" and "two-bit hustlers who would do anything for a buck." Yet these two controversial figures may be the gurus who will lead America into the Golden Age.

Boodle and Scheckel's success story began in the Summer of Love, 1966, when they met on a cancer research project in San Francisco. "I was rationing out cigarettes to the rats, and Georgia was collecting the butts for analysis," Sheckel recalls. "For this we went to med school? The *real* experiments were going on outside: mind-expanding drugs, free festivals, free love..." Quitting their respectable laboratory jobs, Boodle and Scheckel began exhaustive research on the new sexuality.

Their first innovation was "pay love." In Boodle's words, "Rolling in the mud at rock concerts was fine for hippies who didn't know any better, but what about the middle-management dude who didn't want to ruin his Nehru jacket? To him free love was worth nothing. But 'pay love'—there was a concept he could relate to."

On the basis of this discovery the two scientists found sponsors who helped them start their own research facility off the freeway in Encino, between a used-car lot and a Jack-in-the-Box. The avowed purpose of the Center for Creative Carnality was "to help clients overcome their sexual problems scientifically." With their staff of surrogates (unlicensed masseuses from West Hollywood) the doctors pioneered the concept of the Minimum Daily Orgasm and won wide acclaim for their innovative use of sunken bathtubs, inflatable toys, and Cool Whip.

Foundation for Fiduciosexual Fullfillment

For over ten years the clinic prospered, but in 1979 the two researchers noticed a disturbing trend. Waiting-room copies of *Playboy, Sexology,* and *American Nudist* lay untouched next to worn, soiled editions of *Barrons, Business Week,* and *Forbes.* Patients refused to let go of their wallets when they undressed. According to Scheckel, "The clincher was our best customer, who jumped off the table in the middle of a heavy massage and told his surrogate, 'Sorry, honey, but it's time to call my broker.' That's when I realized we'd have to change to keep up with the times." Suddenly money was sexier than sex itself.

In order to "go with the cash flow," Scheckel and Boodle moved to Palm Springs to open the posh Foundation for Fiduciosexual Fullfillment. Here, in oversized, carpeted safe deposit boxes, they help clients "get in touch with their money."

"It's all strictly over-the-counter," insists Boodle. "Everything we do here is in accordance with generally accepted principles of accounting—even the double entries. Our books are always wide open."

But is cash therapy really necessary? Aren't people capable of loving their money without professional help? Boodle and Scheckel maintain that most people still have a low "cash consciousness" and view money as a passive "thing," something that "just lies there" rather than as a divine instrument sensitive to every touch of the "invisible hand" and the miracle of the marketplace.

"We want our clients to overcome their fear of finance," Scheckel explains. "All their lives they've heard that certain forbidden financial practices cause bankrupture, insolvency, or unwanted issue. We teach them to let go of the old double standard and let the gold standard into their lives!"

A look through the foundation's files reveals that certain fiscal dysfunctions are surprisingly widespread. The following queries from insecure investors range from the penny-ante to those which threaten economic existence itself.

Cost Overrun

Dear Doctors,

I can't control my spending. When the desire to consume comes over me, I whip out my wallet no matter where I am. Often I end up with something I didn't need or even want. Does anyone else have this problem?

"Cap" Weinberger, Department of Defense

Dear "Cap,"

Uncontrollable spending is one of the most widespread but risky financial practices today, especially in the military. If you overindulge, you may wake up to find your balance sheets covered with red ink, in which case you should cease all economic activity immediately. Breathe deeply and repeat the money-tree mantra—"The check is in the mail, the check is in the mail"—until your inflation rate subsides. If the condition persists, consult your personal banker or visit our clinic.

Trickle-Down

Dear Doctors,

We've heard a lot about "trickle-down" lately. What exactly is it? I'm confused.

David Stockman

Dear Dave,

Trickle-down is an embarrassing condition characterized by subnormal cash flow. The sufferer fears his or her liquidity depends on the whims of the better-endowed. Trickle-down victims are particu-

larly vulnerable to recession, depression, and Republican administrations. They develop strange phobias, such as fear of pink slips and rubber checks. Many appear pale and overdrawn.

Short of massive injections of liquidity, little can be done to build their confidence. One well-known cash therapist reports promising results with the "nickel-and-dime approach," which encourages the patient to seek satisfaction with his or her own hidden resources. One client, whom I'll call A., went through all his pockets, drawers, and piggy banks and achieved enhanced self-worth by rolling his nickels, dimes, and pennies.

Frozen Assets

Dear Doctors,

I have suffered for several quarters from frozen assets. What can I do? I never had trouble achieving liquidity with any of my previous investments.

Evangeline Gouletas-Carey

Dear Evangeline,

A freeze is one of those things that can happen to anyone's money at any time, but fortunately the condition is usually reversible. You yourself may have caused the problem. Wanting your money sup-

ply to be safe, you locked it up with long-term in-struments. Now that you want and need your funds, they are frozen, and no wonder. You must stay in closer touch with your money if you want it to be available for your immediate needs.

Portfolio Envy

Dear Doctors,

I love my money, but lately I've been losing interest. Other people's assets seem more attractive. I've always been security-minded, but lately I've had recurring fantasies of plunging back into the money market and playing it for all it's worth. This would involve breaking a personal trust, and I might even stand to lose everything, but I just can't get it off my mind.

Robert Vesco

Dear Robert,

You should seek counsel from your securities analyst or an officer of the Fidelity Bank before making any rash investments. Consider the sad story of B., who thought that all his income was dis-posable—a not uncommon delusion in our modern throwaway society. One day B. would be flush with cash, the next painfully overextended. His economic affairs ultimately left him (and his capi-tal) exhausted. Unable to invest anything on a long-term basis, or even to meet his short-term obli-gations, he fell into a depression which has never bottomed out. He wanders the corridors of our clinic, begging to be liquidated. There is no known cure, but early auditing by experienced analysts when this condition is in its first quarter is the key to treatment and prevention.

16

Diminishing Returns

Dear Doctors,
    As a father and a union man, I'm troubled to find that the more I work for my money, the less it works for me. It just doesn't seem fair. What can I do?

Lane Kirkland

Dear Lane,
    Your money may be overtaxed. Nowadays everyone expects his money to go out into the marketplace and work, but at a certain point diminishing returns set in. Should this occur, you should shelter your money or send it abroad for a while. Also effective—and enjoyable—is the practice of rolling over one's investments from time to time. You and your money are just a little tired of each other. Bringing new life to old assets is a challenge but well worth the creative effort.

Card Carrying
(compulsive)

Dear Doctors,
    Consumption used to frighten me, but now that I have credit cards, my pent-up demand has become a flood. Now I can get my hands on desirable consumer goods without surrendering precious cash, and it feels so good I'm afraid it must be wrong. Is it "kinky" to be into plastic instead of the real thing?

Karl Malden

Dear Mr. Malden,
There is abso-
lutely nothing wrong
with using a credit
card, but remember it
is merely a surrogate.
If you come to depend
on it for daily spend-
ing, your cash flow will
suffer in the long run.
Those easy monthly
payments will get har-
der and harder, and
soon you won't be able
to get up any cash.
Handle your credit card lovingly but wisely.

Clerical Error

Dear Doctors,

Deep in my heart I lust after hard currency,
but I come from a deeply religious family, in which
the word of the parish priest is taken as gospel.
He insists that money is the root of all evil and that
it is harder for a rich man to get into heaven than
for a camel to pass through the eye of a needle.
This sounds painful! Isn't it possible to do good by
doing well?

Jerry Windfall

Dear Jerry,
Gilt, not guilt, is the name of the game. Did
you ever check out the ring the Holy Father wears?
Did you ever get a glimpse of his sumptuous
sanctuary? Did you know that he has been speculat-
ing with Church funds? Your Father is into fi-

nance up to his rosaries. If he can get with it, so can you!

Woolgathering

Dear Doctors,
All my life I have paid for things in cash, and in turn have been paid in cash. The green stuff used to excite me when I held it in my hand, but lately I've been fantasizing about using something different, like, for instance, sheep. After all, sheep are warmer and cuddlier than bills or coins. Am I a "sickie" who needs professional help, or have I just missed my calling as a shepherd?
"Bo" Peep, 10

Dear Bo,
You are expressing a desire to barter, *which is perfectly normal and nothing to be ashamed of. Barter goes back to ancient times, as evidenced by such primal myths as that of Jason and the Golden Fleece, and was considered the highest form of economic intercourse by the great Greek philosophers. Don't let a bunch of budgetary bigots make you feel sheepish about getting wild and woolly.*

Loss of Interest

Dear Doctors,
Lately I get no enjoyment out of worldly

19

things—they just seem to weigh me down. Could it be I have sated my desire for wealth and position? Perhaps it is time to divest myself of all my worldly goods and go begging in the streets for rice. Can a person find true spiritual fulfillment without money?

Sid Arthur
Croton-on-Ganges, India

Dear Sid,
  No.

The doctors' advice has helped many to take the first step toward economic recovery, but for full fiduciosexual fulfillment an intensive and expensive course of treatment at the foundation is indicated. Boodle and Scheckel point with pride to their results—"Over 100,000 Served"—and to dramatic case histories like that of Candace K.

When Candace arrived at the clinic, she didn't even know where her money was. "It's only money," she said. "Why keep track?" Under hypnosis she admitted that she had "never gotten off on it," was tired of "faking interest," and hadn't been "getting any" for years. Her Standard & Poor rating measured way below standard—in fact, poor.

In spite of these liabilities the doctors sensed in Candace a potential for deep investment. They worked to build her underdeveloped reserves of confidence and to upgrade her Mental Business Attitude, or MBA. To these ends they prescribed the following fiscal and mental exercises, which anyone can do safely at home in only fifteen to thirty minutes a day.

Fiscal Exercise Program

PROBLEM AREA	EXERCISE	RESULT
Tight money	Dollar stretch ($10/day)	Greater flexibility
Falling profits	Skimming (1 cash register/day)	Takes a little off the top
Capital drying up	Juggling figures (5 columns/day)	Bulging portfolio
Low money supply	Putting the squeeze on (300 lbs. pressure/day)	Improves circulation
Soft demand	Kickbacks (5 envelopes/day)	Sounder footing
Hyperinflation	Business cycling	Better budget balance
Sagging economy	A run on the bank (5 miles/day) or A random walk (10 miles/day)	Sound dollars

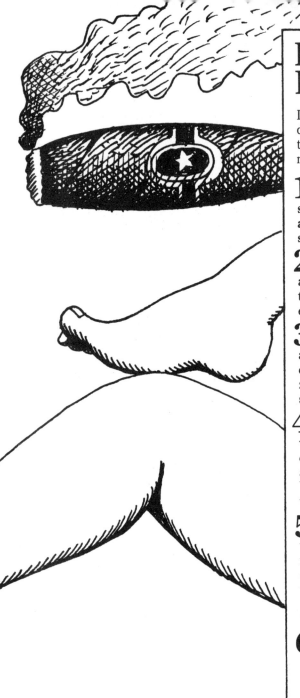

Financial Fantasies

In order to heighten Candace's perceptions of **realty**, the doctors also recommended fantasies like these:

1 Remove your clothes, sit behind a big desk, puff a fat cigar, and give yourself a raise.

2 Remove your clothes and write yourself a letter from your banker increasing your credit line.

3 Remove your clothes and practice writing huge checks. See how many zeros you can fit into the space provided.

4 Buy a rigged roulette wheel, remove your clothes, and pretend you are "the house" at a Vegas casino. Then roll in the chips.

5 Whenever you see any valuable real estate, remove your clothes and say to yourself in an authoritative tone, "Self, someday this will all be yours."

6 Paint your brick fireplace gold, remove your clothes, and climb inside Now pretend you are alone in Fort Knox.

Cash therapy worked for Candace. After achieving a Mental Business Attitude, she returned to work as a legal secretary and began typing herself into all the firm's most important wills. When several wealthy clients died, Candace spirited their money off to Acapulco, where she enjoys it to this day.

Boodle and Scheckel's achievements alarm some sociologists, who recently speculated about the societal implications of the Mental Business Attitude at a "futures" conference. Their predictions, projections, and wild guesses present a dizzying array of options. Some of the questions raised:

Will the obsolete family unit be replaced by the holding company? Will formerly stable partnerships go public and engage in active trading? Will men or women bring home the bacon, and will it be in the form of pork belly futures? Will the parenting of children be phased out in favor of the parenting of companies? Will scientists finally give man the means to "take it with him"?

The only certainty today is that the Fiduciosexual Revolution will bring about no small change in our values, and that no one will remain exempt.

CHAPTER TWO

WHAT DOES MONEY WANT?

Getting a Feel for Your Assets

How to Look Like a Million Bucks: The Dress for Excess Program

Money—eternally desirable, infinitely precious, vitally necessary to us all—remains an enigma to even its most ardent pursuers. Is currency hard or soft by nature? Is cash really cold? Does money talk, and if so, what is it trying to tell us? Mankind has long sought to unravel the mysteries of *das ewiges Finanziell,* the Eternal Financial, for in order to attract and hold money, one must first understand it. Although no single theory can possibly account for its volatility, many have been advanced and some have gained currency in ecoanalytic circles.

Ecoanalysis was born in Vienna one Friday afternoon in 18__ , when Sigmund Freud found himself waiting in an interminable bank line. Suddenly a despondent depositor grabbed his arm and asked whether his money could possibly be saved. At the time, Freud himself had failed to achieve a reconcilation with his money. He threw up his checkbook and posed the now-famous question: "What does money want?"

In Freud's time men valued money but treated it as a commodity, a passive chattel. Flashing it in public was frowned upon, so it was kept at home, forbidden to venture into the public marketplace. Money enjoyed security. It was admired for its surface glitter. Yet despite its sterling reputation, money was prone to wild fluctuations, sudden panics, and inexplicable depressions. Some money became withdrawn and dwindled away to nothing. Freud resolved to analyze money, to account for the awful toll this sort of life was taking on it.

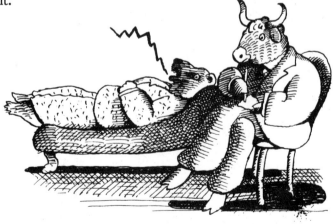

First he took one (1) thin pfennig from his pocket and laid it gently on his couch. It expressed such profound debasement and self-depreciation that Freud felt poor just looking at it. Then he surrounded the pfennig with bills and coins of all denominations, and instantly it brightened up, its worth increased substantially. "Evidently, money likes money," Freud observed, "but how does this alter its relations with us?"

Freud haunted the local streets and shops, scrutinizing the movements of money. Sitting in a café, he observed a man with a tin cup, openly pleading for money to come to him. At that moment a stack of bills sashayed past him in the hands of a waiter, who gave it to the gentleman at the next table. The gentleman stroked each bill and slipped it beside the many others in his wallet, where it rested comfortably. "Now I see," wrote Freud, "why you've got to have money to make money. Alone, a bill or coin is insecure, but the company of money increases its sense of worth."

Freud then sought out the places preferred by money, following it into countinghouses, bank vaults, and deep pockets hitherto unexplored. He toured the "money belts," capital-intensive neighborhoods like the financial district and the Upper East Side of Vienna. So far his theory rang true, but where were the indicators leading?

One night, laboring over his tax return, Freud hit the jackpot. Of course, the vastest aggregation of money lay in the coffers of the government. With great excitement Freud wrote on the back of a receipt: "What does money want? Money wants to combine

with money in an ever-growing stream, to flow with great velocity back to the primordial source, the one who gave it life: the Mint."

Ever since, men have sheltered their money carefully, lest it stray back to the governmental womb. One analyst in particular, B. F. Skinflint, owes Freud the greatest debt. Skinflint contends that his money gives him no quarter, and in its zeal to escape will even burn a hole in his pocket. He holds his money in check by locking it in a box, never touching it: a severe penalty, reminiscent of the barbaric custom of "burying treasure." Skinflint boasts that he really has a hold over his money, that it can never leave him. But what a price to pay. Stifled thus, money cannot achieve a normal rate of growth. It becomes dull and unyielding, and its anxieties compound daily.

Modern money wants and needs the freedom to become productive in society, as most mainstream ecoanalysts now recognize. Capital now ventures out to work, circulating freely and developing its own interest. However, as a result its behavior has become increasingly capricious. Money jumps from pocket to pocket with astonishing velocity, leaving one man for another without a backward glance. Unscrupulous "Cashanovas" entice the bills from our thin wallets into their ample ones. Forceful "macho" types manhandle our money while we watch in horror. Americans are crying all the way to the bank, and ecoanalysts' offices are jam-packed with distraught patients (and large portions of their money). The most prevalent complaints: "My money doesn't go as far as it used to." "I can't make enough money." "I'm losing my money." "Someone is stealing my money from me."

What will we do? What *will* we do?

This crisis of confidence has spawned some fraudulent analytic trends, particularly in Washington, where fringe ecoanalysts practice whatever the market will bear.

During the Great Society years "income transference" enjoyed a brief vogue among the elite. They collected in a small room and "threw money at problems." The problems, mostly welfare recipients, resented being pelted with coins and called the cops. The money felt equally ill-used. Today the bureaucrats "throw problems at money." They blame their poor job performance on the inadequacies of the money they have to work with. But money soon tires of this buck-passing. It hates bad news, and when it is subjected to endless tales of woe (like presidential speeches), it loses confidence and tightens up. Not even a State of the Union massage will help it loosen up and go with the flow.

Tight Money.

An equally bankrupt theory is offered in Dr. Wane Dire's *Your Erroneous Bank Statement.* Here Dire asserts that he can change his money and make it responsive to his every desire. Dire is begging the question here. Money resists change and in extreme cases must be "broken down," a painful ordeal involving the purchase of an unwanted newspaper or candy bar.

Fortunately one new approach—Transaction Analysis, or T & A—is starting to pay off. According to T & A, money keeps us guessing by playing different roles in different transactions. For example Joe lays his bottom dollar on the table during a poker game. Suddenly it moves away from him and becomes Mike's fast buck. Joe is hurt and confused. T & A explains that the dollar's dual personalities are merely two sides of the same coin. That dollar's real value, or RV, *was, is, and will always be one hundred cents,* regardless of its role in the transaction.

Most of us take money at face value. We pursue empty stereotypes, blind to the RV of the rest of the world's money supply. For example some people are attracted only to *borrowed money.* They frequent places like the Money Store because they get a charge out of "paying for it." Those accustomed to the genteel society of *old money* write off *new money* as tasteless and vulgar. And the saddest cases of

Front Money?

all squander their lives in pursuit of *easy money.* They chase it around racetracks, casinos, and stock exchanges, always trying to score. But *easy money* never returns their interest, and soon they are wildly throwing *good money* after *bad.* T & A teaches us to stop cheating ourselves, to open our wallets to all denominations and appreciate each for what it is: money.

RECOMMENDATIONS FROM THE LATEST
T & A MARKET LETTER

Good money: hold	**Bad money: cut your losses**
Smart money	Mad money
Seed money	Dirty money
Front money	Funny money
Walking-around money	Hush money
Pin money	Blood money
Money to burn	

Ecoanalysis and You

Ecoanalysis has brought countless spenders out of their slump and given them a new lease on life. You too can capitalize on its benefits.

First, pause and take stock. When you're holding a nice round sum, does it slip through your fingers? Is the feeling between you and your funds really mutual?

Or do you have inflated expectations? The cause of inflation was once thought to be "too much money chasing after too few goods," but these days there are "too many people chasing after too little money," particularly in our urban centers. You may complain that there is a shortage of unattached assets, that all the good money is already taken. You have probably been looking for money in all the wrong places, like those "singles" bars. Don't cheapen yourself by picking up loose change. Go to the "money belt" in your town and join a worthwhile cause, like soliciting charitable contributions. Soon, with a little trust, you will be holding the money you dream of.

Be patient. There is no quick fix. And remember, no man truly *possesses* money: he only holds it for a time. Someday you may have to part with your money and close the books, but meanwhile spend your time together wisely.

Your money will have its ups and downs. At times you will have to make allowances for its liabilities, but over the long term you will be richly compensated. As you and your money mature, a bond will grow between you, and you will know the contentment that only a security can provide. For in the final analysis money was put on this earth to give man pleasure, and all it *really* wants in return is interest and appreciation.

How to Look Like a Million Bucks: The Dress for Excess Program

First impressions are important. To attract money, even the most understanding lover must first dress the part. Take your cue from Liberace, Cher, the Mandrell Sisters, and other wealthy entertainers, who invariably wear outfits with the sleek, shimmering look of gold and silver. The more you look like money, the more money will like you. For inspiration study the fashion examples on the following pages.

Conservative

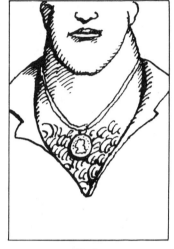

Macho

Rock

Punk

Military-industrial

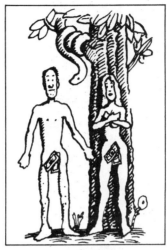

Original

Traditional

Ridiculous

CHAPTER THREE
BULLS DO IT
BEARS DO IT

MANIPULATING MONEY
THE WALL STREET WAY

You and your money may have always enjoyed a satisfying relationship with Fidelity Trust, but sooner or later you'll wonder: Is that all there is? You become hungry for a little excitement. Your eyes often wander over the stock quotations in the paper, and you find yourself fantasizing about all that action on the Street. What really goes on under the counter, behind the discreet facades of its famous "houses"? Surely it would be safe to plunge just once...

Only those "in the life" know how the fast-paced rhythm of the Street can get into your blood and take over. The most hardened Street pros (or "brokers," in the colorful Street lingo) were once—like you—just looking for a quick score. One of them, "John," tells his sordid life story to anyone who will listen, including this reporter.

37

A rainy Monday on the Street, 9:50 A.M. John nervously adjusts the sharp lapels of his Brooks Brothers suit. Lately his volume has been sluggish, and he's hungry. Nearby, a few insiders nod over the morning gold fix, keeping an eye peeled for "bears" (colorful Street talk for the cops). John stakes out his positions warily. Last week the bears almost busted him for public tender solicitation.

John is a dedicated hustler, first in, last out in every business climate, but now the years of heavy trading are taking their toll. John looks washed-out, a faded remnant of the glamorous highflier who electrified the Street in the sixties. Like so many others, John ran away from a jerkwater business school to pursue his dreams of limitless options and a gold future. He never intended to stay on the Street. He figured he would trade on his assets while he was at his fiscal peak, then cash out and settle down in the suburbs.

John was initiated in the back room of a popular "go-go" fund, a swinging outfit that went both long and short.

As he explains, "We matched up customers with the day's offerings. Some clients are looking for a sweet thing that's just gone public, others prefer a more seasoned performer, you know? So we eye-balled all the figures, studied the curves. You look for a well-defined head and shoulders, a smooth, rounded bottom, a plunging V-formation—then you call the client, and if the price is right, they get together."

John developed a keen eye and impeccable taste. Quickly he built up an "active list" of outstanding high-grade issues. His customers included judges, politicians, bank presidents: men with important, high-pressure jobs who occasionally felt the need to release their pent-up demand. They contacted John discreetly by phone or through intermediaries, and John delivered. He became adept at satisfying every marginal propensity.

One Friday the go-go fund was raided.

"There was a scandal," says John, "something to do with salad oil. I had to slip out before taking a bath. The bears closed us down, and there I was, pounding the pavement. My back was to the wall. But I still had my active list and lots of phone numbers, so I rented some rooms and started a little house of my own."

John furnished the house with velvet drapes, white shag carpeting, and cushions of cash. He soon had a stable of aggressive young customer's men working for him, back-and-forthing twelve hours a day with private clients. The house's services came high, but John provided the "blue-chip specials."

The Heavy Industrials

"Our customers were an odd lot," muses John, absently stroking his wallet. "One, a barrel-chested oil man, was dying to plunge into heavy industrials. I got him Bruce Tool and Die, a top-heavy number in a dominant position, but the guy was a transvestor. He didn't have the means to perform. Last I heard, he'd gone to Switzerland to have his portfolio restructured."

His favorite client, John recalls, was a distinguished older man with an almost federal reserve, who had suffered a painful tax bite in a very vulnerable spot. For months all he could do was peek through loopholes. He felt excluded, until he came to John.

"All the guy needed was a little pump priming. Almost overnight he turned into a wild swinger, getting into simultaneous positions on both sides with Dynoflex and Flexodyne here."

John took out a dog-eared snapshot.

"Check this out. That's called a tax straddle butterfly spread. Yes, it's hard to keep your balance, but if you're in shape, it's fantastic. Just don't try it if you have a weak ticker."

The grateful client offered John a joint venture and an unlimited line of cocaine, and John's business soared to an all-time high. But in his euphoria he did the one thing that no Street pro should ever do. He fell for a hot new issue, Simultronic Vibrolator. He was wild about that adorable saucer bottom, that upside potential, those undulating curves. This was the one he wanted to hold and support for the rest of his life. Quarter after quarter he waited for his darling to yield to him. Nothing. But he held on through its harrowing surges and collapses. One morning the news of Simultronic's forced liquidation flashed over the wire.

John's bubble had burst. He went into a decline. Now he knew that if you're a Street hustler, you can't afford to invest yourself. That's strictly for the herd, or in John's words, "nothing but bull."

He threw himself into a frenzy of upside action. Trying to forget, he found himself indulging in unsafe and unsound practices.

"One night an associate talked me into trying a little bond-swapping," John confesses. "I really didn't want to—I mean, most of those bonds hadn't even reached maturity. Just as we were pulling off their coupons, the vice squad broke down the door. I tried to hedge my position, but I couldn't cover my shorts in time."

From jail John put in a call to his favorite client, who quickly posted bond. But out on the Street things were heating up. John's flagrant manipulations had churned up a lot of resentment in the investment community. A powerful broker, known for prompt, accurate executions, had put out a contract on his life. Worst of all, John feared he had consumption. Friends advised him to consult a specialist and keep a low profile.

John decided to seek shelter the only way he knew how. He bought a tropical suit on margin and cruised the floor, hoping to snare himself a "cash cow" (the colorful Street term for a wealthy and undemanding benefactor). That day trading was off sharply, but right before the closing bell he caught the eye of a fatherly, gnomelike financier who was interested in a little discreet arbitrage.

Cash Cow

John's cash cow liked to invite a few like-minded old bondholders into his leather-paneled library, where they rolled over their positions and after a few brandies occasionally subordinated some debentures. John introduced them to some beautiful short candidates and serviced their mortgages (when necessary). In return John's cash cow showered him with Krugerrands. He took him to the Hamptons by helicopter, to the squash club by Rolls-Royce. And on John's birthday, he presented him with a bulging portfolio of gilt-edged utilities, enough to set him up for life.

Meanwhile John's old friends on the Street were hearing bearish rumors—John has plummeted to an all-time low, he's been wiped out, he's cashed in his chips. But one day John suddenly surfaced on the Street, looking better than ever with his new Guccis and alligator attaché case. He has remained on the Street ever since.

"I'm a hustler," he says defiantly, "and that's all I'll ever be. Who needs security? It's a big bore. I almost lost my mind in that mansion, with those old geezers clipping coupons all day. The Street is where the action is. This" —he gestures toward the teeming buyers and sellers, the brokers, the in-and-outers— "this is my life, it's all I know. It's my stock in trade."

The Annual Report

by Shere Annual

Since Kinsey countless scientists, anthropologists, and voyeurs have poked around in America's bedrooms discovering much, perhaps too much about human sexuality. But next to nothing is known about what goes on in America's boardrooms. After all, a corporation is a person too, an intricate conglomeration of delicately balanced feelings which have been privately held—until *The Annual Report.* In response to our confidential questionnaire thousands of companies have lifted the corporate veil to reveal their intimate desires and practices. Here in their own words they talk about *merger,* their own and the institution in general.

Question 1: Why did you merge? Are you satisfied with your merger partner?

Of the corporations who answered this question, a staggering 82 percent were merged, and a mind-boggling 74 percent find their mergers satisfying. In spite of the recent increase in the divestiture rate, merger remains a viable way of life. However equality in merger is still rare. In an astounding 91 percent of mergers a large powerful company takes over a smaller one and exercises complete control. Predictably the acquiring companies (a huge 97 percent) enjoy merger more than their more vulnerable targets (a pathetic 33⅓ percent).

Why do companies merge? A shocking 62 percent say, in the words of one oil company:

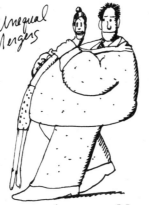

Unequal Mergers

"Everyone in my industry had merger plans. It was the thing to do, so I did it."

A remarkable 16 percent merged in order to become parent companies:

"I like the warm feeling of nurturing my little subsidiaries, watching the brother and sister companies grow. Merger has made me fully integrated."

Many struggling young companies look to merger as a way out of a crisis, while some merge to advance their ambitions:

"Before my present merger I was way below par. My previous suitor did a fast turnaround and skipped town, leaving me in a sensitive cash-flow position. My sinking fund was sinking fast. So I slimmed down and went to a broker at Morgan, Stanley, and Yenta. He arranged an exploratory meeting with an extremely friendly old conglomerate, loaded with cash. That very night I opened my books to him, and between the balance sheets we discovered assets I never knew I had. He didn't

mind my liabilities; in fact my losses made me all the more attractive to him. Together we achieved deep market penetration, and soon we were merged. So far it's the best thing that's ever happened to me."

SHOES TO CADILLACS

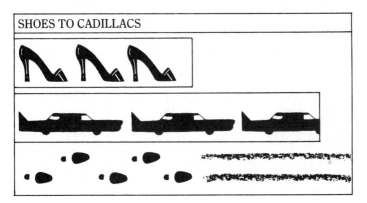

"Back in my small midwestern town I dreamed about joining the Fortune 500, *with their private Lear jets, glittering penthouses, and lavish expense accounts. But how could a tiny shoe factory gain entree into high society, except by making a brilliant merger? Luckily my bottom line caught the eye of a blue-chip corporation, who took a controlling interest in my affairs. Of course he's much older, but he's a good provider, and for our anniversary he gave me a convertible."*

And a few companies, mostly savings banks, merged because they "had to:"

"I was a goody-goody, always thrifty and willing to help the small investor. But somehow I got in trouble. Fortunately I was insured for up to $100,000, and my uncle put pressure on the other bank to go through with a merger. I'm a little

ashamed that my merger was arranged, but my uncle says we'll learn to love each other."

PROFILE OF AN ATTRACTIVE CORPORATION

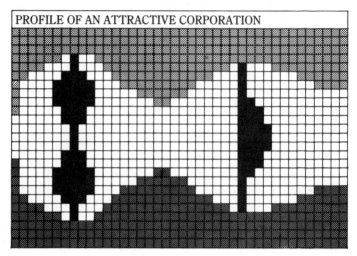

Question 2: If you have never merged, why not? Do you plan to merge in the future?

O f companies never merged, an amazing 89 percent say they would merge if they found the right partners:

"These young companies today just don't know a good thing when they see one. I'm well positioned, with ample credit lines, but I can't seem to find an appealing merger prospect. They all insist on equity and refuse to change their names. Call me an old fogy, but when I merge, I'll be the one who takes over, and my partner will be my wholly owned subsidiary."

> *"I'm still testing the market. I receive many unsolicited tender offers, but they seem so unfriendly. These suitors just want to get their hands on my assets. If they think I'm for sale to the highest bidder, they're wrong. Call me an old-fashioned girl, but I'm willing to wait until my White Knight comes along."*

Fully 37 percent expressed reservations about merger, particularly the loss of autonomy:

> *"I've never merged because I prefer to pursue diversified interests. I've been involved in joint ventures with companies all over the world, some of whom remain close friends. Right now I have an interest in several attractive companies, but not more than 9.9 percent in any one of them. Maybe when my assets begin to depreciate, I'll take a partner, but she'll have to agree to an open merger."*

Question 3: If previously merged, what caused your breakup? Would you merge again? If so, why? If not, why not? If undecided, why can't you make up your mind?

Divestiture is definitely on the rise. Of the extraordinary 28 percent of the companies whose mergers failed, an unsurprising 100 percent were bitter and confused:

> *"After seven years of merger my partner wrote me off. I feel drained. Whatever reserves I had are*

exhausted. Before he slammed the door, he said he only wanted me for a preacquisition net operating loss carry-forward. I don't understand it."

"Everyone calls me 'Ma,' so when I gave up my little subsidiaries, it caused a scandal in the papers. Actually they all live a long distance away and can operate without assistance. I raised them well, with no hang-ups. And I'm not going to cut them off without a dime. Every Sunday I reach out and touch them for three minutes, and that's plenty. When they were little, I put my career plans on hold, but now that they're gone, I'm getting into the computer field."

"My ex-partner found horizontal integration distasteful. I tried the straight-line method, the flow-through method, but nothing helped. Every time I removed her financial underpinnings, she froze. I began to approach outside suppliers, seeking an outlet for my excess capacity. Ultimately we split, and she got most of my shares.

"Merge again? I wouldn't foreclose the possibility, but only if our capital structures are compatible."

50

Unwanted Issue

51

Conclusions: The institution of merger is clearly here to stay, but for most of our respondents it is far from perfect. In the future we may see fewer mergers and more divestitures. As small companies become adept at thwarting unwanted advances, the old-style predatory suitors will have to sweeten their offers or even woo by proxy. Partnerships will expand more slowly, thanks to improved financial planning devices. Incompatible companies will split, not stay together for the sake of their subsidiaries.

But with more trust and less antitrust many companies will make lasting mergers. The happiest, most successful mergers will afford both partners the chance to grow and diversify in perfect synergy.

PLAYDOUGH

BANKBOOK SIZE —
IS IT REALLY
IMPORTANT?

BONDS IN BONDAGE

MONEY OF THE
MONTH: THE
EURODOLLAR

PLUS EXCERPTS FROM
PAPPY TALESE'S "THY
NEIGHBOR'S WALLET"

THE UNITED STATES OF AMERICA

In an exclusive excerpt from his explosive new book Happy Talese explores America's money mores and finds that "the way to a man's wallet is through his pocket..."

Thy Neighbor's Wallet

by Happy Talese

I t was a dark and stormy night. Happy Talese, a middle-class, middle-aged married man who always wears a suit and tie, sat in the bar of the Conventional Arms Hotel researching his monumental study of capital and conscience in America. He was thinking about the two typical Americans from whom he had just extracted embarrassing revelations of anguish and passion. A pattern was coalescing in Talese's insatiable mind: Despite the Fiduciosexual Revolution middle-class Americans remain repressed when it comes to the only detachable part of the human anatomy, namely, the wallet. To display one's wallet openly is a provocation; to touch another's wallet, a violation. After all, one's very identity and power spring from the folds of one's wallet, as the story of Raymond D'Agostino clearly shows.

D'Agostino, a twenty-nine-year-old middle manager from Parsippany, New Jersey, left his wallet in a jacket which his wife, Doreen, took to the One Hour Cleaners. It was the worst one hour of Raymond's life. For all practical purposes he ceased to exist. He could not pay the paper boy, drive to the mall, or charge a Popeil Pocket Fisherman to a convenient toll-free number. Worst of all, the man at the cleaners would soon be privy to his most intimate secrets: his parking transgressions, his bookie's unlisted phone number, what he and Doreen looked like in high school. Raymond felt helpless, humiliated, naked. His hyperactive mind flashed back to his first wallet, a tooled leather billfold which he had stitched together with plastic string in Arts and Crafts at Joe Namath Football Camp in 1965.

Suddenly Doreen burst through the back door, brandishing Raymond's wayward wallet: "Hey, stupid, you left this in your pocket!" Raymond's hour of hell was over. He was once again a fully functioning middle-class American male.

As Talese pondered Raymond's traumatic experience his hand slipped furtively into his pants pocket. Talese often felt the desire to pull out his wallet and reassure himself that its contents were adequate. He removed it slowly, shielding the contents from view. As a boy he had often awakened at night to empty his piggy bank and count the coins. But even then he possessed the overpowering compulsion to investigate other people's hidden lives that would ultimately drive him to journalism. One day, seeing his mother's pocketbook open on the sofa, he reached in and removed her wallet, To this day he can see the red vinyl, the plastic compartments, the S & H Green Stamps, the $5.52, and the first-grade picture of himself, Happy Talese. Afterward he felt sick and ashamed and wrote a 25,000-word article about it for his school newspaper.

Talese absently stroked the soft leather of his billfold, the smooth credit cards, the crisp bills. His restless thoughts turned to Barry Krauthammer, whose strange story hinted at ecstasies far beyond the traditional confines of wallet-centered activity.

Barry Krauthammer, the forty-four-year-old president of Acme Hanger and Shoehorn, slammed the door of his Cordoba and walked disconsolately to his bachelor apartment. *Another evening shot to hell,* he thought, picturing the luscious blond divorcée who had refused to accompany him home. And another walletful shot to hell: parking $7.50, cocktails $13.45, dinner $75.98 with tax and tip, play $60.00, nightcap $8.52. As Barry peeled off those twenties, she had gazed at him with rapt adoration, but now both his bed and his wallet were empty.

"To her I'm nothing but a wallet," he muttered as he kicked off his Guccis. "Well, to hell with her, it's her loss."

As Barry walked into his walk-in closet his frustration gave way to mounting anticipation. Instinctively he reached for a shoebox on the top shelf and opened it. His fingers eagerly gripped the contents, so familiar and soothing to his touch. It fit so comfortably in his hand: $2,000 in fifty-dollar bills, neatly stacked and stapled together. Slowly, expertly he removed the staples and caressed each bill, rubbing it against his cheeks and neck. Soon he had forgotten the divorcée, the wasted evening, his depleted wallet.

"You're mine, all mine," he whispered, spreading the bills out on his water bed...

Talese gasped. How lucky he was to find such indiscreet subjects to interview. At this rate his book would write itself. Mentally he began counting his royalties and stacking them in shoeboxes. Suddenly a noisy group burst into the bar, jolting him out of his fantasy. To Talese's horror he recognized them as the Walletchinskys, led by Irving Wallets, the only author in America with fatter books and a fatter wallet than Talese himself. Talese felt threatened and hurriedly shoved his wallet back into his pocket.

Wallets slapped Talese on the back. "Hey, Happy, how's your book? We just sold our latest, *The Wide World of Wallets,* to *ABC Sports.* Here, have a round on me," he said, producing a wallet the size of an eggplant.

Talese slumped face down on the bar. Several young Walletchinskys swarmed around him, patting his head, his shoulders, his pockets. Before Talese could cry out, a hand insinuated itself into his hip pocket, crept around his wallet, and *(continued on page 158)*

PLAYDOUGH QUIZ

How Fiscally Stimulating Are You *Really*?

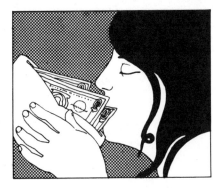

Sure, you're attractive (or you wouldn't be reading this fabulous magazine!) but do you possess the magic magnetism that makes a person irresistible to capital? Take this revealing test and find out. Even if you've never pictured yourself as a potential Rockefeller, you may discover a lucrative libido you never *dreamed* you had. Check the answer you *honestly* agree with, using your favorite #2 pencil. The results may *astound* you!

1. You enjoy being the center of attention:

    a) at a Tupperware party
    b) in a public lavatory
    c) at a bankruptcy hearing
    d) in Howard Hughes's will

2. When E. F. Hutton talks, you:

    a) tell him to shut up
    b) ignore him
    c) listen
    d) get excited

3. You run into an old flame whom you haven't seen in years. You:

    a) reminisce about that wild weekend at the Shady Acres Motel
    b) point at his toupee and laugh
    c) ask him for a large amount of money

4. The business of America is:

    a) none of your business
    b) out of business
    c) monkey business
    d) business

5. You take your money to the bank and the teller manhandles it. You:

    a) offer to count it yourself
    b) challenge him to a duel
    c) avert your eyes and cry
    d) plead with him to be nicer to your money

6. To give is:

    a) better than to receive
    b) a mistake you'll always regret
    c) a fate worse than death

7. A fool and his money are soon:

    a) to be a major motion picture
    b) parted
    c) a thing of beauty and a joy forever
    d) indistinguishable

8. In the middle of a party you go upstairs to the bathroom and notice that your host's safe is open. You:

    a) lower your voice and say, "Excuse me, but your safe is open."
    b) point rudely when his back is turned

c) enjoy a few private moments
with his money, then close
the safe

d) stuff as much money as you can
into your pockets, shoes, and
underwear, then rejoin the party
as if nothing had happened

9. The best things in life are:

a) easily affordable
b) fungible
c) available only by prospectus
d) green

10. Which of the following is
a perversion?

a) golden showers

b) Keynesianism
c) whipping inflation
d) getting a little on the supply side

11. Sometimes during lovemaking you
close your eyes and pretend you are
really with:

a) Robert Redford
b) Milton Friedman
c) David Rockefeller
d) a debenture

To find out your score and the key to
your personality, just send $9.95 plus
postage and handling to Lew Lucre,
publisher, *Playdough* magazine.

Mark Eden Capital Development

Before

After

Do people point at your portfolio
and laugh? Are you taken advantage
of by your insurance salesman,
cheated by your butcher, and short-
changed by the ice cream man? Do
you constantly lose money to pay
phones and cigarette machines? You
need MARK EDEN'S CAPITAL DE-
VELOPMENT!

The MARK EDEN plan turned
pathetic Willard Wimpley into a Wall
Street wunderkind in only seven
weeks, and helped him acquire a
bulging portfolio. How can YOU
achieve ample assets in just fourteen
hours a day? Just send for our FREE
booklet and find out.

(Please enclose $9.95 for postage and handling.)

PLAYDOUGH CENTERFOLD: THE EURODOLLAR

Our current Money of the Month is an international star, the toast of
six continents: the irrepressible Eurodollar. This frisky American
beauty is uninhibited, unregulated, and hard to hold.
She winters in the Cayman Islands, summers in Switzerland, and
makes flying visits to central banks all over the world. The
Eurodollar is always in demand, but she's so elusive that few have
ever actually seen her. But here she is, captured by *Playdough*'s
camera in a rare moment of repose.

THE INSATIABLE INVESTOR

Best Banks—
Where the Money Is

At its best, banking is an adventure. The right bank can excite even the most jaded investor. But to find the most interesting service you've really got to shop around. *Playdough's* Insatiable Investor hit the road in search of a full range of banking experiences. The agony and the ecstasy of banking is shown in its full glory in his survey of some of the best (and *worst*) banks in America today.

Bank:	Imaginary Invest-ment and Loan
Access to Funds:	Through your subconscious mind
Interest:	Intellectual and intense
Service:	Officers always ready to talk money
Decor:	Elegant
Atmosphere:	Hushed, reverent, quietly dignified
Hygiene:	Cleaned out

While most banks place an emphasis on tangible assets, *Imaginary's* motto is "It's all in your mind." If you like carrying figures in your head, this is the place for *you*. Understanding loan officers are always available to sit and swap fantasies, gossip about the exploits of money-about-town, or reminisce about the "first time"—that piggy bank you shared your bed with, that lucky coin that stayed in your pants for

months. No subject is taboo. For those who prefer privacy, *Imaginary's* tantalizing telephone tellers "give good phone"—they're ready to talk money *anytime*. The crystal chandeliers, oil portraits of glaring robber barons, and tasteful wood paneling all recall a lost era when the bank actually had money.

Bank:	First Sabine Women's Bank
Access to Funds:	Easy, far too easy
Interest:	Savings receive Tender Loving Care
Service:	Intimate, laid-back
Decor:	The turkish harem look
Atmosphere:	Redolent with perfume
Hygiene:	Approved by Board of Health

Sabine certainly lives up to its reputation as "The bank that bends over backwards." While all customers' loan applications are readily approved, the bank is even more generous to armed strangers with stockings over their heads. You can get at your cash easily, but it can be abducted at any time. *Sabine's* Easy Virtue and Soft and Yielding Accounts are tempting, but can you really trust a bank that's such a pushover?

Bank:	Progressive Farmers and Livestock

Access to Funds:	Customers must milk own cash cows
Interest:	Unnatural—resources increased through animal husbandry, shepardizing, etc.
Service:	No horsing around
Decor:	A stable environment
Atmosphere:	Pungent aroma; difficult to breathe
Hygiene:	Appalling

The pork belly future is **now** at *P F & L*. Their "high-on-the-hog banking service" is not for those with weak stomachs or a strong sense of smell, but if you're looking for dirty money, this is the place. Hold your nose and take a gander at *P F & L*'s make-hay-while-the-sun-shines investment programs and their fox-in-the-henhouse mortgage loans. Rumor has it that this is Miss Piggy's bank.

Bank:	Freeway Interstate Drive-In Bank of California
Access to Funds:	Nonstop, express service
Interest:	Compounded instantaneously
Service:	Rush
Decor:	Turnpike Modern
Atmosphere:	Choked with fumes
Hygiene:	Eat my dust!

For a quickie try "The fastest bank in the West." Although exact change is not required, it does help speed depositors through the tellers' area. Customers must throw their money into a basket to get the green light on their transactions. However, many complain that even at the withdrawal window they aren't given time to count, let alone caress their money. It is difficult under these circumstances to have a meaningful banking experience.

Bank:	Penny-Saver's Nickel-and-Dime Thrift & Loan
Access to Funds:	Pocket money only, from coin dispensers
Interest:	Meager
Service:	Penny-ante
Decor:	Threadbare, Thrift-Shop Bleak
Atmosphere:	Thin (the cost of oxygen is going up)
Hygiene:	Spotless though shabby

A holdover from preinflation days, when a penny saved was a penny earned. The bank's "coins only" policy results in low yields and excruciatingly slow transactions—one careless gesture can cause a major spill, halting business for hours. Still, the constant rolling of quarters, dimes, and nickels excites the bank's regular customers. "I enjoy being stingy with myself, and here at *Penny-Saver's* they let you do that," said an anonymous millionaire. "*Penny-Saver's* isn't just a playground for the poor."

Bank:	Seamen's and Mechanics' Manly Bank
Access to Funds:	Haul away anytime
Interest:	Hearty

Service:	Rough, ready, muscular
Decor:	Industrial, nautical
Atmosphere:	Salt, sweat, and Old Spice
Hygiene:	Minimal

Whether hefting bags of money across their ample shoulders, wrestling with your credit problems, or hoisting up your interest rates, *Seaman's and Mechanics'* backs up your money with a lot of muscle. These are men's men, who earn your interest with the sweat of their brows—in fact, they perspire heavily just thinking about your money. Your funds are safe, though. If any mechanic or sailor is found dallying with your dollars, every man jack of them is flogged. Embezzlers are keelhauled.

Tattooed, bare-chested guards check your ID before letting you have at your hard-earned cash. "Going down below, are ye?" the men leer, bursting into hearty laughter. Their economic exuberance is contagious.

Bank:	Sinking Fund Savings and Swim Wear, The Old Swamp Shopping Mall, Landfill, N.J.
Access to Funds:	High liquidity, snorkel required
Interest:	Level rising hourly
Service:	Wet and wild
Decor:	Suburban Mildewed
Atmosphere:	Moist, gaseous
Hygiene:	Condemned by Board of Health

A visit to this bank can dampen the spirits of even the most acquisitive. The tellers are muddy-headed at best. "A bank built on a sanitary landfill site just can't get good help nowadays," the man-ager burbled to me through the muck. "It's hard enough just to keep our heads above water." Such premiums such as snorkels, fins, and bathyspheres have failed to lure back depositors. Funds are soggy, but the bank promises to introduce a drip-dry dollar. The future profits picture remains murky.

There are other banks you might find worth visiting. If you are partial to petrodollars, The Oklahoma Crude National Bank just might put a tiger in your tank. If you like to live dangerously, try the Double-or-Nothing Lucky Savings Bank in Jackpot, Nevada, where a nickel can turn into $10,000 in less than an hour. (Of course, $10,000 can also turn into a nickel in no time flat.) Hot air is at a premium at Inflatable Savings and Loan, "The Zeppelin Bank," where soaring interest rates keep your money aloft. Zeppelin is flying high right now, but beware of long-term investments. Analysts predict the bubble will soon burst.

If you are interested in more in-depth information, send $9.95 to the Insatiable Investor c/o *Playdough* magazine, and we will send you the full-color booklet *How Does Your Bank Stack Up?*

Coming next month, "Foreign Money—Better in Bed?" If you have a yen for money of other lands and want to make a mark in foreign exchange, you can't afford to miss this column. The Insatiable Investor takes a franc look at the krone, weighs the pound against the zloty, and examines the frantic peso of Latin banking. The Insatiable Investor will also answer the age-old question: "Do liras make lousy lovers?"

PLAYDOUGH INTERVIEW: JARVIS HOWARD

While a former B actor took Washington by storm, another politician quietly slipped out of town to head for the bright lights of Hollywood. Jarvis Howard, the three-term ultraconservative congressman from Boiling Blood, Arkansas, had decided to turn his skill for bombast into box-office bucks. Raised by Bible-thumping, God-fearing parents, Howard had made a political career out of fearing God and thumping Bibles. He is famous for his tirades against taxation, job safety, poor people, and women. (On the fair sex he is quoted as saying, "I think we should send them all back where they came from!")

Playdough tracked the wily ex-pol to his Beverly Hills retreat to quiz him on his political reputation and controversial career switch.

PLAYDOUGH: You first ran for Congress on an independent line, didn't you?

HOWARD: That's right, the right-to-blight party. I was backed by some local industrialists who felt that raw sewage was getting a raw deal. The regulatory monster in Washington was trampling all over market freedoms, and the spendaholics both Democratic and Republican kept pouring money into the bottomless pit of the public sector like drunken sailors on a binge. It made my blood boil!

PLAYDOUGH: What did you do about it?

HOWARD: I took aim against the money moochers with a proposal to cut taxes by 100 percent, thus drastically reducing the size of government.

PLAYDOUGH: But how would the country run without big government—without, in fact, any government at all?

HOWARD: Better, much, much better. Private enterprise would fill the gap.

PLAYDOUGH: But what you're proposing, isn't it a little like the withering away of the state described by Marx?

HOWARD: Are you calling me a commie? Only a commie would call Jarvis Howard a commie! I'm an *American*!

PLAYDOUGH: Please, Mr. Howard, calm down. I'm only trying to clarify your controversial views for our readers.

HOWARD: Okay, but you better not start any of that commie stuff with me again. I hate commies! They smell bad and don't believe in God!

PLAYDOUGH: Okay, okay, but getting back to the point, what about Defense?

How would we defend our country without any tax revenue?

HOWARD: Again, private enterprise. Different companies could sponsor their favorite branch of the military in their market area. Regiments could bear the name of their corporate sponsor: the Kentucky Fried Colonels, or the White Cloud Toilet Paper Airborne Division. Mr. Clean could sponsor the mopping-up operations.

PLAYDOUGH: This sounds fascinating. *Playdough* might even be interested in getting involved on the procurement end. But moving right along, what about your sponsorship of the controversial EWA (Eliminate Women Altogether) amendment? What inspired that?

HOWARD: Aah, all they do is nag, nag, nag. I don't need some female to give me a sense of self-worth. I'd rather have a fiduciosexual fling, slipping around with my slush fund. With no women around we'd have more free time to make love to *our money*!

PLAYDOUGH: Why are you leaving politics?

HOWARD: The money. Out here I'm more bankable. When my favorite director, Michael Breadwinner, offered me the lead in *Tax Attack: Washington*, I jumped at the chance.

PLAYDOUGH: Of course your recent censure gave you added impetus.

HOWARD: Of course.

PLAYDOUGH: Mr. Breadwinner's other films—*The Spendathon Man, Cool Hand Loophole,* and *Hog-Wild Pork Barrels of Washington*—have been rather explicit. Will you have to strip your assets for the camera?

HOWARD: I've been promised my stunt double will do all that dirty stuff.

PLAYDOUGH: Is it true that there are scenes involving economic discipline?

HOWARD: Well, there is one excruciating scene where the bad guys tighten the money supply, constricting circulation and strangling investment opportunity.

PLAYDOUGH: Sounds brutal. But the good guys play pretty rough too, don't they?

HOWARD: Only out of righteous anger. For instance, my character ends a huge Washington spending orgy by taking a wrecking ball to the EPA, the HEW, and OSHA.

PLAYDOUGH: I've heard that the climax is pretty startling too.

HOWARD: Oh, yeah, that's the scene where we whip inflation *once and for all*!

PLAYDOUGH: Well, we're all looking forward to seeing *Tax Attack: Washington* at our local theaters. Thank you.

HOWARD: "Thank you"—is *that* all? Are you trying to stiff me out of that check you promised?

CASH REGISTERS
OF THE GODS
IN SEARCH OF ANCIENT ACCOUNTANTS

by Erich von Mannikin

Stodgy scientists still insist that man developed through the boring process of evolution. But what of ancient cities built overnight? What of pyramids with tellers' cages and chambers filled with treasure? What of the gaming tables and unearthly velvet paintings found in a South American cave? These cannot be explained by existing theories. There is only one *possible* explanation—that *gods* from *outer space* issued galactic loan guarantees to underwrite civilization as we know it!

A system of speculation, sexual favors, and banking extending far beyond the solar system has existed for millions of years. I have found the receipts, bankbooks, and checks chiseled in stone to prove it! Yet world banking authorities refuse to examine my evidence, or even cash my checks.

They ignore me at their peril. For these tablets, figurines, and trinkets (*chatchkas,* in archaelogists' argot) all tell the same story: Ancient accountants were here. They're coming back. And they want their interest.

What brought the ancient accountants to Earth? We may speculate that a shake-out at their celestial headquarters sent them off in search of new assets to strip. This is the basis of the story of the Flood in Genesis. An account which more accurately places this event on another planet can be found in "Origin of the Superman" (Action Comics 1, 1939.).

The Bible tells us that "the sons of God came in unto the daughters of men, and they bore children to them." This was a cash transaction, which not only introduced the use of money, but created the world's oldest profession—a great step forward for human culture. Sports and bets placed on sporting events were also introduced, for "there were Giants in the earth in those days." Ancient stone carvings of football-helmeted figures confirm this. Pyramid-casinos built by the Egyptians to alien specifications came soon after. There is unassailable evidence that Ezekiel's "wheel" belonged to a roulette table. Nefertiti was definitely an alien, as her high-tech headset indicates.

The influence of the gods was generally beneficent, but they could be wrathful when provoked. Sodom and Gomorrah were both torched for refusing to pay protection money. The Tower of Babel was destroyed when it refused to go co-op.

My earlier exposés—*Bad Checks from Outer Space* and *Go-Go Funds of the Gods*—explain all this. But what of the devastating flight of capital to **other planets**? Astronomical sums totaled up in flashing lights in the sky, the jingling of coins overhead, and receipts showering down on major cities all over the world? These events can mean only one thing! The ancient accountants are back! Vast withdrawals have already begun. I need not tell you that this will have earth-shaking effects on our balance of payments.

These sightings are not "marsh gas" or "weather balloons," as the Federal Reserve would have you believe, but cash registers of the gods, chock full of unidentified flying assets. **Our** assets!

The recent upheavals in economics, politics, and situation comedy can all be traced to the "long green men." Ask yourself—who elected Ronald Reagan? Is "Iron Lady" Margaret Thatcher actually a robot engineered by illegal aliens? Who blew up Mt. St. Helens? Who shot J. R.? All these events can be attributed to extraterrestrials! Unprecedented increases in inflation, unemployment, and poverty are the inevitable result of this capital flight to the stars.

What can we do? Run and hide. We are powerless. I'm holed up in my basement with my life savings in gold, a fifty-year supply of oatmeal, and an antiaircraft gun. Those who do not kowtow to traditional explanations will see my point. I leave it to the scientific world to answer to me.

COMING NEXT MONTH

Spending Orgies—
How to Get Invited

Playdough **Interview—**
Milton Greedman
The frisky free marketeer and friend of shady South American governments talks frankly about economic discipline, whipping inflation, and his new TV series, *Free To Use.*

The First Time—Your palms were moist, your eyes glistened with expectation. Do you remember your first allowance?

The Cashless Society — Curse or Blight? *or Why I Can't Get a Charge Out of Electronic Banking*—Editorial by Lew Lucre, Publisher

CHAPTER SIX

THE
SMART MONEY
An Academic Approach

Fig. 1 Monetary units of speech

Many narrative works, both classic and obscure, are not the conventional love stories they seem, but thinly veiled tales of "that which surpasses the love of men or women"—the love of money. The analysis of art and literature for hidden financial symbolism is called *fiduciotics.* Professor Claude Argent-Monnaie virtually invented the science of fiduciotics with his seminal essay *The Role of Spare Change in Literature,* which traced the literature of money love from the sunny innocence of *Jason and the Golden Fleece* to the dark, brooding modernism of *By Cash Possessed*, from the classic Indian text the *Kash-a Sutra* to the present-day *Joy of Cash*. Monnaie's theories are also the basis of the new monetarist school of film criticism.

Fig. 2 Jason and the Golden Fleece

The essay we have chosen is a brief explanation of fiduciotic theory and methodology from Argent-Monnaie's self-acclaimed masterpiece *Myth/Cliché/Certified Check,* as yet unpublished due to lack of funds.

*T*raditional criticism has always wrongheadedly approached narrative as "story" rather than structure. In order to apprehend the narrative "house," one must first analyze the "bricks" it is made from—and the structural cement which holds them together. On the linguistic level these units are wordomatic—the paragraphomat, the sentensorama, and the wordeme. On the metalinguistic level, however, these units are monetary. Such expressions as "stop sticking your two cents in" or "stop nickel-and-diming me" are not merely idiomatic, they are central to the psychology of language (at least to the psychology of *mine*). Literary passages can be broken down into basic fiduciotic units (the ten-dollar word, the five-dollar word, the penny for your thoughts) and further analyzed for their precious metal content. Here is a typical breakdown of a passage from *By Cash Possessed*:

Katrinka's hair fell down on	
the velvety smooth skin of	*velvet $40/yd.*
her back like a golden shower.	*gold $350/oz.*
Her diamond eyes sparkled.	*diamonds $20,000/karat*
"My treasure,"	*estimate unavailable*
Ivan Silverubelovich	*silver $6.60/oz.*
	ruble 64 percent on the dollar
murmured, drawing back the	
satin sheets.	*satin $5.50/yd.*
"You are worth more to me	
than all the tea in China,	*oolong tea $2.20/lb. (warehouse)*
all the	
masterpieces in the Louvre,	*$1,000,000,000,000,000*
all the stars in the sky."	*estimate unavailable*
Playfully she grabbed his	
silver zipper	*silver $6.60/oz.*

*T*he microeconomic approach yields a vast reward of literary insights. First we see that there is little "hard" money in this passage. Such overt economic eroticism would not yet be acceptable (or redeemable) in a nineteenth-century novel. However, this passage is suffused with soft-currency symbolism, both lyrical and lucrative. Like some baroque bank statement, the book's luxurious prose only reveals its full worth if one invests the time necessary to draw it out. "One must strip away at the penny-ante aspects of a work…to mine for the riches within."[1] It has long been known that some works reward the reader more than others, which could easily be taken out of circulation. Presses employed to churn out such paltry works as *Poor Relations* and *The Hunger Artist* and playscripts such as *Curse of the Starving Class* could be better employed to print bank notes, leases, and book contracts for brilliant but unappreciated French academics.[2] The most worthwhile literature is that which can be analyzed not only word by word but also paragraph by paragraph and chapter by chapter, revealing larger fiduciotic themes. When shopping for true literary value, one must be sure the whole is greater than the sum of its parts.

Like most reputable critics, I favor a tale that involves "a fortune hunter, a fortune, a scantily clad

---

1 Lionel Shilling, *Mining for Meaning in Modern Literature*, p. 999, Pretentious Press, $19.95 plus tax. Shilling, who was paid by the page, once wrote a hundred-page essay on the word *the*.

2 See my essay *Pedants, Publishing's Persecuted Minority*, in the July 1980 issue of *Academic Angst Magazine*. (Incidentally I have not yet received a sou from the editors for this piece. *"La checque, c'est à la poste,"* indeed.)

female, and people beating each other up,"³ However,
I will settle for any story in which the main character
has a hoard of cash, such as *A Christmas Carol*.

Fig.3 Money has made a rich contribution to art as well as literature. Leonardo per Capita's *Still Life with Paper Currency*
shows the early influence of Mercantilism on Renaissance
painting.

A Christmas Carol is one of the most misun-
derstood works of modern literature. Traditional critics treat it as a warmhearted fable rather than a tragic
tale of decline and fall. A closer reading of the work reveals a story not of moral uplift but of a forthright, hon-

---

3 See Albert Moocow, *Tough Guys Fight Dirty*, printed in its entirety in
my collection *Idiotexte*, Vanity Press, 1966. A tightfisted publisher and
rampant academic philistinism have kept my anthology from becoming a
standard college text—have conspired, in fact, to keep it out of print and
off university bookshelves forever. However, a laundered version of
Moocow's essay is excerpted in Susan Maytag's *Against Agitation*,
Washday Press, 1967.

Fig. 4 *The Athens School of Business*, by David, Comte de la Rocque-à-fellô. He is also famous for his monumental *Mes Amis de la Chase*.

est, money-loving man buckling under to social pressure. Who has not dreamed of emulating Scrooge and casting off the petty constraints of morality and human decency, of giving his soul over to the voluptuousness of greed? Scrooge is consumed with the compulsion to count over and over each saucy sovereign, and for this he is condemned as a miser and a skinflint. What makes Scrooge heroic? He *acts* on his avarice, unlike the hypocrites who denounce him, who have merely repressed their illicit economic urges. He is an advanced thinker, not a credulous worshiper of "the Christmas Spirit" or the fearsome deity "Santa Claus," who "knows if you've been naughty or nice."[4] He denounces such primitive superstition as exactly what it is—"Humbug!"

Fig.5 Santy

---

4 "Santa Claus Is Coming to Town," music by J. Fred Coots, words by Haven Gillespie. Copyright 1934, Leo Feist, Inc.

What strikes the reader is Scrooge's modernity. Certainly the modern spirit of Christmas owes more to Scrooge's canny commercialism than to Cratchit's treacly sentimentality. *Carol* chronicles Scrooge's failure to transcend Victorian prudery and "love only gold" as a true Nietzschean *Goldenmensch* or, as Fleming calls him, *Goldfinger.*

Fleming's book better fits my requirements for a modern novel. It has not one but several well-endowed but barely dressed women. One is even painted completely gold to heighten the forbidden fiducioerotic thrill the hero feels when he unites with her. It is like possessing gold, like "marrying money." Goldfinger himself approaches the ideal of the heroic hoarder. Just as Scrooge is a repressed Goldfinger, Goldfinger is a fully realized Scrooge figure. [5] As he tells his nemesis, that formidable symbol of financial prudence, James "Bond":

> "All my life I have been in love... with gold. I love its color, its brilliance, its divine heaviness... [its] soft sliminess. I love the warm tang it exudes when I melt it down into a true golden syrup. But above all, I love the power that gold alone gives its owner."

Who could be closer to his money than Goldfinger, who "carries a belt full of gold coins around

---

5 Other Scrooge figures include King Midas, Rumpelstiltskin, Charles Foster Kane, Long John Silver, King Tut, and fugitive financier Robert Vesco. See *The Treasure in the Text: The Scrooge Figure in Fact and Fiction* and *Savings, Sacrifice, and Redemption in the Eighteenth Century Novel,* by Simon Simoleon, published by Tightwad Press.

his stomach" and "thin [gold] sheets in the bottom and sides of his suitcases"? Goldfinger's heroic lust cannot be contained by the narrow conventions of commerce, by timid men who think "the safest way to double your money is to fold it twice and put it in your pocket." He must do what no man has ever done—make love to all the gold in Fort Knox. Because the prudish powers that be find his fiscal fascination repellent, he is forced into a life of crime to gain the object of his affections. Condemned for his transgressions against the Treasury, he is hunted down and liquidated by Bond, a paid lackey of the public sector.

Goldfinger's unhappy fate is not shared by the contentious college-town couples in Edward Allsaver's *Who's Afraid of Bernard Baruch?* Allsaver's plot, based on a true story in *Barrons,* is as eternal as the theater itself: a brutal evening of capital-intensive games (Devalue the Dinner Guests, Destabilize the Department Head, and Penalize the Professor) undermines fidelity and trust and results in illegal combinations, with near-tragic consequences. Just as things look bleakest, with both partnerships tottering at the brink of bankruptcy, the characters revaluate their positions, withdraw their illicit tender offers, renegotiate their mutual bonds, stop competing, and incorporate. George and Martha finally achieve the parenthood they have longed for—as a corporation. The younger couple start over again on a sound basis. This happy ending is a breakthrough in the portrayal of fiduciosexuality. While the taboo against showing people loving money onstage had long since been broken, amorous acquisitiveness had previously been portrayed as a liability rather than an asset.

*T*he cinema's treatment of similar subject matter has been characteristically lighter, prime examples being George Lukor's *Philadelphia Mutual Story* and his musicals *High Finance* and *Seven Bribes For Seven Brothers. Seven Bribes,* featuring a famous score by Countem and Greenback and a complete backlot recreation of the public and private sectors, may be the most lavishly financed musical of all time. [6]

Fiduciosexuality in music surfaced during the Great Depression, with blues such as *Buddy, Can You Spare a Dime?* and more fiscally stimulating songs like *We're in the Money.* But it was the savage rhythm of rock 'n' roll that unleashed a pent-up flood of liquidity in America and abroad. After a sneering, leering Elvis Presley begged his bank account, "Love me tender," the world could never be the same. [7]

In the academic world, fiducioticians have received no credit for their discoveries, let alone accreditation. Years after the Fiduciosexual Revolution swept college campuses, a cruel double standard still exists:

---

6 The fascinating inside story of this Mucho-Golden-Moola production is told in Raymond Ducat's exhaustingly researched *Dollar Signs and Symbols in the Cinema.*

7 See Georgia Gildersleeve's great treatise on bioeconomics, *Wealth and Puberty.*

SEVEN BRIBES FOR SEVEN BROTHERS

it is all right to love your money, and even to live with it, but only if you keep it "under the mattress." Those who "do it" aren't supposed to talk about it, and those who talk about it lose their tenure as well as their tender.[8]

Booksellers, librarians, and my own publisher have proved even less enlightened. They have forced me to buy back (at cost) every copy of my last book, *The Significance of the Insignificant in Everyday Life*. This classic text is not available in any store. How much would you expect to pay for such a major oeuvre? But wait, don't answer yet! For, if you write now, I will include at no extra cost *The Book Contract As Literature: A Closer Reading*. But that is not all! For a limited time only, I will also send the mystical masterpiece SECRETS OF THE ECONOMETRICIANS. These secrets are known only to a few and understood by none. Master them and your life will be changed. Just send $9.95, to L'Ecole Fiduciotique, Box 500, Paris, France, or dial 800–M-O-N-N-A-I-E (in New Jersey, MOney Hill 7–1000) and charge it.

With your help my research can continue until the ideas I have expressed here become common intellectual currency. For my arguments are as sound as a dollar. No matter what cultural information I appraise and decode, it always adds up to the same thing—*"la monnaie, c'est tout!"*

---

8 Once, in anger, I asked the president of a great university, "Is it, then, that all money is dirty?" He smiled wanly and replied, "Of course—if it's any good!"

CHAPTER SEVEN

THE WAY OF THE

D'OW

While American businessmen desperately pore over obscure Buddhist texts, samurai epics, and dog-eared copies of *Shōgun* in search of the secret of Japanese management, their Eastern counterparts are beating the pants off them by following the teachings of an American named Henry Jones. After years of apprenticeship with the greatest masters of the "hardball" school, Jones emerged as an entrepreneur of evangelistic fervor and Zenlike calm. His synthesis of Eastern and Western techniques forms the basis of the "can-do" school of martial money management.

A champion proxy fighter and tax dodger, Jones was considered unbeatable in courtroom, boardroom, and barroom brawls. No litigator or regulator could hold him, thanks to his unique use of the "loophole," "steamroller," and "great-escape-clause" techniques. Just weeks before his death the invincible Jones retired to a rec-room La-Z-Boy to add up the accounts of his capital-intensive life. There he dicated the almost-mythic tome known as *The Way of the D'ow.*

By combining many forms—the pep talk, the aphorism, the instruction booklet, the as-told-to biography—the D'ow transcends category. It is an all-encompassing body of knowledge. From it, even the novice can learn how to achieve ecstatic union with the Almighty Dollar and become the "One with All."

Meetings With Remarketable Men

THE WANDERER

The early life of "the Jones" remains shrouded in mystery. Other students at Middlington's Average Normal School remember him as "that squinty-eyed kid I gave my milk money to for safekeeping" and "that guy who convinced me to swap my comic book collection for a municipal bond." Jones's restless, acquisitive spirit soon led him away from home, to the Path of Panhandling. One day, while wandering through the Texas Panhandle in search of others of his kind, he fell into despair. "Beer money and pocket money will never add up to the BIG money!" he cried out. In a flash of insight he realized he needed a mentor, a numismatic leader to show him the road to riches. But where would he find him? It was then that the weary mendicant raised his eyes and beheld a fiery sign of the purest neon, which read:

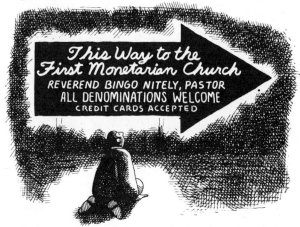

The church itself little resembled that in Jones's hometown—it looked a good deal more like a bank, and the preacher wore the three-piece suit of a banker. Most important, Reverend Nitely spoke a language Jones could understand.

When Nitely spoke of the Great Redeemer, whose coming was long overdue, and the leading indicators that showed his interest and his eventual guaranteed Return, he touched Jones deeply. And when he turned to Profits 1:8 and read, "Now is not the time to lose faith... a vast Reward for all his children will trickle down from the clouds, as pennies from heaven," Jones knew he had hit the jackpot. He begged to be taken into the fold. Seeing that the youth had the "Barracuda-nature," Nitely signed him up as a full-time disciple.

Jones's interest compounded daily. He learned to cure the possessed by removing their possessions, and how to heal people's bankbooks by the laying on of hands. He enriched the lives of young widows through the Reverend's Undressing/ Blessing Plan.

Driving the Money Changers from the Temple to the Bank

This idyllic period proved short-term. Nitely's unorthodox preachments aroused the wrath of the strait-laced religious and investment communities. All in one horrible day he was defrocked, stripped of his credit rating, and indicted for tax evasion. His heavily insured church was burned to the ground, either by a heavenly thunderbolt or by a suspiciously lit fire (accounts vary). Nitely and Jones were forced to flee into the wilderness. It was apparent the world was not ready for this new teaching.

84

THE LOST YEARS

Jones's history after the Flight out of Texas becomes hazy. Certainly his famous commentaries on *The Accountant's Book of the Deadbeats* date from this period. Jones was deeply impressed by the Book's harrowing account of the Day of Reckoning, when all tabular matter is toted up and those with debts outstanding are trebly punished with reclamation, amortization, and liquidation. M. O. "Skip" Tracer of the Karmic Debt Collection Agency of Ventura, California, may have introduced Jones to these sacred scrolls before sending him out to be "a fisher of lost sous."

Jones's ability to draw blood from a turnip, water

Camel Training

from a rock, and cash from the cashless was the stuff of legend. But the worship of other Collectors and a modest salary were not enough to sustain him spiritually, and once more he went abroad in the land to seek his Reward. The Miracles of the Marketplace (raising the debt, turning stock into water) and the famous Sermon on the Mint date from this period. Jones later rejoined Nitely at his Higher Realty Co., where he sold Incorporeal Properties: 6 RMS HVNLY VU, NR RT HND OF GD, CONVT. TO RAPTUROUS TRANSPT. The slogan "Can't afford that Mansion in the Sky? Try our Condo in the Clouds!" is generally attributed to Jones. As his sloganeering improved he grew bored with the door-to-door approach. When he read of the advent of Sri Baksheesh, whose staff worshiped him as "the Advatar," opportunity beckoned. Jones hastened to Madison Avenue to join Sri's Tantric Advertising Agency.

THE ADVATAR

Baksheesh's innovative kash-and-karma approach (based on the idea that "a sucker is reborn every minute") had turned his tiny kashram into a gold mine. New talent was attracted by Baksheesh's seductive personality and the alluring philosophy of the Four Unique Selling Points and the Noble Billfold Path:

"Learn to master the passions—not your own passions, but those of others. The undisciplined mind is like a runaway horse. You must lead this horse to water and make it drink. That more - than - one - beer thirst, once stimulated, can never be quenched, for its name is Desire. This is the secret of tantric advertising—it ignites but does not extinguish, arouses but does not satisfy. Sex energy, instead of being squandered on sex objects, is diverted to luxury objects by using the Four Unique Selling Points: It's new, it's improved, it's guaranteed, and it comes with this special free offer. This in turn brings higher Brand Awareness, Recognition, and Loyalty.

"Always remember that everything is sex. Selling is sex and buying is sex. Taking out the garbage is sex. Chocolate-flavored cereal, mashed potatoes, and wall-to-wall carpeting are all sex. You can make love to a car, a coffee maker, anything! The entire universe and all bodies earthly and celestial are ruled by the Desires. And thus it is that all things are Good— Good enough to be marketed."

Using Baksheesh's principles, Jones stimulated impulse purchasing, unloading such products as Swansong's freeze-dried chicken parts and Priapique masculine hygiene spray. He surpassed even his mentor at inspiring housewives and husbands alike to "be here now" at the "point of purchase."

The time had come for Jones to seek his own path, but he hesitated, waiting for a message from above. At last it came in his pay envelope—a pink slip which read, "All things are impermanent in this World of Illusion. Please clean out your desk by Noon. Sri."

In advertising, Jones had learned that a product's value resides not in its superficial attributes but in something intangible—some Quality with which it imbues its owner. Using this principle, he founded Intangible Assets, Inc. Jones characterized his product as "software for the soul, microchips which reprogram the human biocomputer through simple transubstantiation." The chips came in four flavors: Wisdom, Pizzazz, Charisma, and Sex Appeal. Except for Wisdom they sold like hotcakes and developed a reputation for Quality. Intangible's Group Mind Department specialized in telepath sales and astral market projections.

Eager investors were never turned down, thanks to Intangible's "pyramid-powered" franchising arrangement. "Our operating principle is that there is so much money in the world you can take all you want and it doesn't matter," Jones told a meeting of the Future

Fat Cats of America. Unfortunately his egalitarian vision was not shared by the big-government bureaucrats in Washington.

One day Jones shocked his followers with an announcement. "I have taught you all I can," the Master told them. "The time has come....Your next and hardest lesson will be self-reliance." He then vanished "under a cloud." Trials and tribulations filled the days ahead. The rumor that astronomical sums had been siphoned off into the spirit world by Akashic Accountants undermined investor confidence, causing further capital flight. Corporate credibility was dealt a deathblow when IA's books were opened to the feds, revealing that all records had been kept in an "invisible hand." Unable to keep retailers "in the chips," Intangible was soon forced to give up the ghost.

Meanwhile Jones had started his "manifest destiny" seminars to give others the benefit of his mystico-managerial thought. For an undisclosed fee he would illuminate the mysteries of "transcendental margin." For an additional fee he would teach the more capitally developed to manifest their destiny through monetary meditation. Having transcended his financial and personal troubles, he began to "rake it in hand over fist" (an obscure fiduciosexual practice detailed in the *Kash-a Sutra*). "Heaven is not up or down...in active trading today," he told his disciples with a cryptic smile. At last his heart (and his lawyers) knew Peace.

The Way of the D'ow
The Teachings

1. THE CALLING

The first step of the Way is the Calling. Money talks, but only to those who choose to listen. There is an indwelling Investment Advisor in all of us, but we must still the inner dialogue to hear him. To fill our pockets, we must first empty our heads, ridding ourselves of feelings of panic, depression, need, and thoughts of overdue bills, loans, and mortgages. Find a place that is without people and suitable for contemplation, such as the inner vault of a bank. Then close your eyes and make of your mind a blank ledger. At once your heart will be filled with an inconsolable longing, your outspread palms will yearn to be oiled, and you will experience a deep sense of emptiness in your pockets. You have reached a higher level of socioeconomic perception. You have been Called to the Way of the D'ow.

2. "CAN-DO": MANIFEST DESTINY IN ACTION

What is "can-do"? It is the art of martial money management—money love in action. It is called "can-do" because anyone "can do it." When you meditate, just visualize a circle of golden light all around you. Within that circle imagine anything your heart desires—a million dollars, a giant palazzo, Sophia Loren. If results are not immediate, do not be discouraged. Only persist, and through "wishcraft" all that you have envisioned will manifest itself. This is the meaning of "manifest destiny."

Can-Do

3. PERSONAL ELECTROMAGNETISM: THE SECRET OF POWER

How can *YOU* achieve capital magnetism? Use the Energies! They are at work all around us—behind our walls, inside our light sockets. When business troubles beset me, I lost that sense of a direct current running through my life. "Who can give me back that positive charge?" I asked. "I can!" a Voice answered from a burning bulb overhead. "Who are you?" "I am Big Allis, Source-of-All-Radiance in the tri-state area, to whom all pay tribute lest they be plunged into outer darkness." "O Fearsome Utility, how may *I* achieve Power?" I tremulously inquired.

"Fear neither the brownout nor the blackout," Allis replied, "nor the meltdown, nor the venting of the steam, for all costs can be passed on to the consumer. This, and only this, is the secret of Perfect Monopoly."

This Good News sent an electric thrill through my body, restoring my capital magnetism. From then on I had the Power to draw money to my side at will.

Profitable Proverbs

"The naked man has little to fear from pickpockets."

"Only strive for the Imitation-of-Chrysler, and your loans shall be guaranteed."

"Demand, and it shall be supplied; knock and the Vault shall be opened."

"I am you and you are me. Therefore entrust me with all you possess—you are only giving it to yourself."

The Final Days

Lately I have been visited in my meditations by visions of a City in the Sky, filled with golden, luminous beings. In these visions I sense that I too am a luminous being. "Where is this rich and wondrous place?" I ask the others. All around are banks of marble and columns of figures rising up into infinity. "Don't you know?" the Voices ask me. "Don't you recognize the Vault of Heaven?" The other day I had my first out-of-pocket experience. I became aware of being lifted out of my body on top of my leather billfold, and gazing down as if from a flying carpet, I saw my lifeless form sprawled across the La-Z-Boy like some immense landscape. All around me I saw my wordly possessions lifting off and following my billfold's heavenward ascent. The meaning of my previous vision became clear to me—you *can* take it with you!! This experience has brought me a deep sense of peace. I have gathered all my worldly possessions together, and I am ready. Only follow the Way I have set out for you, and you can follow me to *your* Just Reward.